211168140

KW-053-689

TS

THE
ARCTIC
AND ITS PEOPLE

Susan Bullen

Wayland

PEOPLE
· AND PLACES ·

The Amazon Rainforest and its People

The Arctic and its People

The Prairies and their People

The Sahara and its People

211168140

Series editor: Cally Chambers
Editor: Book Creation Services
Designer: Mark Whitchurch

Consultant: Dr Elizabeth Cruwys

First published in 1993 by Wayland (Publishers) Ltd
61 Western Road, Hove, East Sussex, BN3 1JD, England

British Library Cataloguing in Publication Data
Bullen, Susan
  Arctic. – (People & Places Series)
  I. Title   II. Series
  998.004

ISBN 0 7502 0487 7

Typeset by Dorchester Typesetting Group Ltd
Printed and bound in Italy by G. Canale & C.S.p.A.

Cover: The village of Morriusaq, in northwest Greenland, nestles in a low-lying inlet of the sea.

Title page: The Norwegian town of Tromsø during the long Arctic night.

Contents page: A fur-clad Inuk uses the latest ski-doo to transport him across the snow.

Acknowledgements
The publishers would like to thank the following for allowing their photographs to be reproduced in this book: Bryan & Cherry Alexander 1, 3, 4, 6, 7, 8, 9, 10(b), 12, 13, 14, 15, 16, 17, 20, 21(a), 21(b), 23, 28, 31, 32(a), 32(b), 33, 36, 38, 44, 45; B&C Alexander/ Wayne Lynch 10(a); B&C Alexander/W. McCloskey 24; BBC Hulton Picture Library 19; Geoscience Features 11, 42; Planet Earth/David A Ponton 27; Science Photo Library 40, 43; Frank Spooner/Gamma 22, 30, 35; Frank Spooner/Shone 39; Zefa 18, 25, 29, 37.

Artwork by Peter Bull 5, 6, 13, 26, 33, 34 and Tony Smith 9, 41.

CONTENTS

▲

Savissivik, in northwest Greenland, is a small village on the barren coast near the ice cap.

*I*magine that you live in an icy wilderness with very little daylight for nine months of the year. In the midst of winter, you will not see the sun for about nine weeks. Now imagine the same place six months later, at the peak of summer. It is carpeted with flowers, buzzing with insects and the sun shines even at midnight. What you have just imagined is the Arctic – a place of sharp contrasts, quite unlike anywhere else on Earth.

There are various ways of defining the Arctic. One way is to include only the lands that lie within the Arctic Circle. Alternatively, we can think of the Arctic as the area north of the 'treeline' – farther north than trees can grow, where there is only tundra and the Arctic Ocean. Some people think that the Arctic is where the land is permanently frozen. And some think it is the area where the warmest temperature is never more than 10°C. In this book, the Arctic is defined as lands in the far north that include Greenland, northern Norway, northern Russia, Alaska, and northern Canada (including the islands that make up the Canadian archipelago). This can be seen on the map.

CLIMATE

Greenland is covered by an ice cap, except for its coastal fringes. The other Arctic lands are mostly free of permanent ice, except for glaciers, although the cold climate ensures that they are snow-covered for much of the year. For eight to nine months of the year, temperatures in the Arctic remain below freezing point (0°C). Temperatures often

Arctic Territory

Take a look at the globe, and you'll find the Arctic right at the top. It is the most northerly part of planet Earth. The Arctic can be defined as the area that lies within the Arctic Circle, an imaginary line around the Earth at 66°33' North. The core of this area is an ice-covered mass of the Arctic Ocean. This ice is permanent. Right in the centre is the North Pole. Away from the North Pole, the frozen sea extends for at least 800 km. Beyond that the sea is only frozen for the coldest part of the year.

The first signs of land appear about 800 km south of the North Pole. There are many small islands, and there is also Greenland – the world's largest island. The northern limits of the huge continents whose territory extends into the Arctic region enclose the islands and the icy seas. The countries which surround the Arctic are the USA (represented by the state of Alaska), Canada, Russia, Finland, Sweden, Norway, Greenland (which belongs to Denmark), and Iceland.

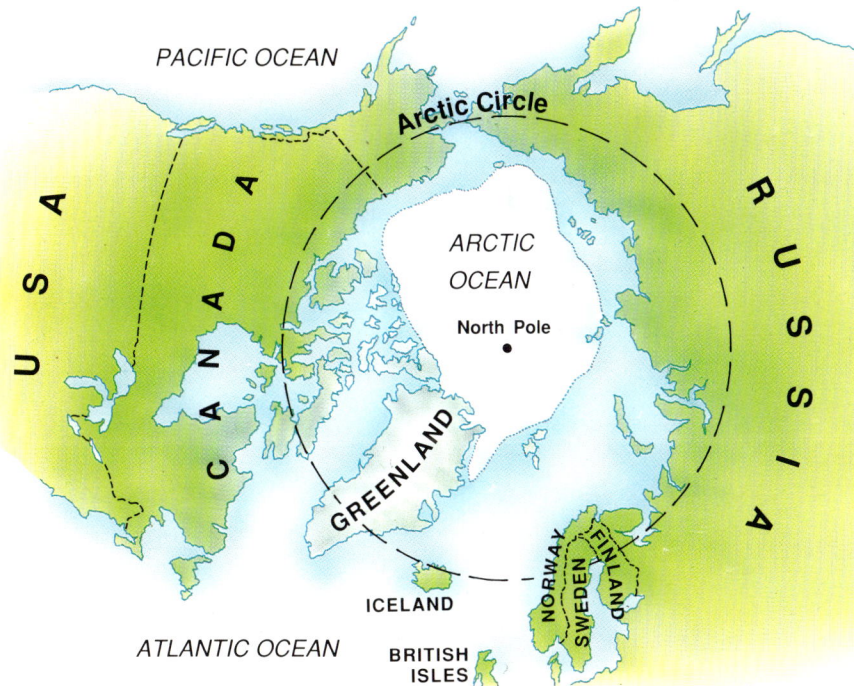

PACIFIC OCEAN

Arctic Circle

U S A

C A N A D A

ARCTIC OCEAN

North Pole

R U S S I A

GREENLAND

NORWAY

SWEDEN

FINLAND

ICELAND

ATLANTIC OCEAN

BRITISH ISLES

reach −40°C. At the edge of the Arctic Circle, however, there are some days in winter when the temperature may not drop below −5°C.

Bitterly cold winds often blow in the Arctic, making it seem even colder. These bleak, wintry conditions last for three-quarters of the year, so the brief Arctic summer is all the more welcome when it comes. In summer, the temperature rarely exceeds 10°C, but a sunny day with clear skies can be very pleasant. In high summer, there is constant daylight, which is why the Arctic is sometimes called 'land of the midnight sun'. This makes a dramatic contrast to the dark Arctic winters, when the sun may not be seen for over two months!

Traditional clothes worn by the Saami include reindeer-skin coats and colourful patterned scarves and hats. These women are in Kautokeino, Norway.

What makes the Arctic climate so extreme? The answer lies in the way the Earth is tilted, which means that the North Pole gets little sunlight for half of the year. When the sun does shine on the Arctic (generally from March to September), it is never directly overhead. Its rays are less powerful than at the tropics, which receive much stronger, more direct sunlight, and so have a warm climate. The large mass of ice and snow plays its part in the Arctic climate too. It reflects much of the sunshine into space, making the Arctic even colder.

ADAPTING TO THE ARCTIC

Naturally, the harsh Arctic climate dramatically shapes the landscape and affects all living things found there. A little way below the ground lies the permafrost, a layer of frozen soil and rock as much as 700 m thick. Above the permafrost, the soil thaws each spring and this allows a unique kind of vegetation to grow. There are no trees, but a dense cover of dwarf, shrubby plants. The region is known as tundra, a Finnish word meaning

barren land. However, the tundra is certainly not without life.

It is not only plants and animals that have adapted to life in the Arctic. People have lived here too, for thousands of years. But no one would claim that the Arctic is an easy place to live in. In this book, you can read about the struggle between the Arctic peoples and the harsh environment that is their home.

The Earth's tilt causes the north pole to face towards the Sun in summer and away from it in winter.

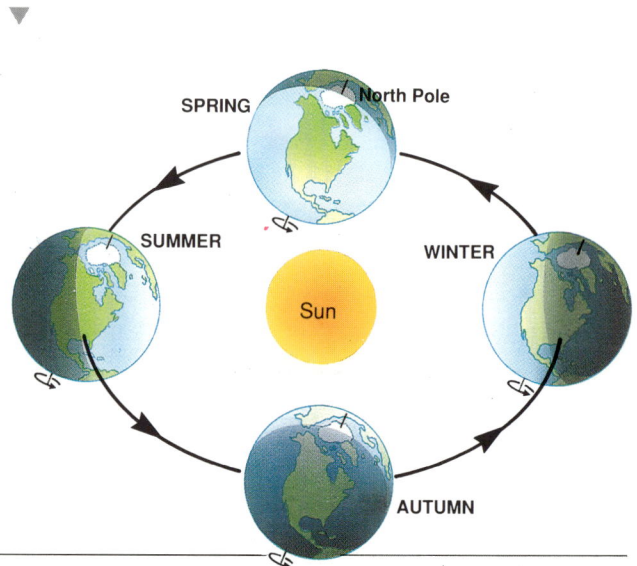

The Arctic is a unique combination of habitats: from the frozen north, ice and sea give way to the tundra, which in turn gives way to the taiga forests that fringe the Arctic Circle. Each of these different habitats supports its own kind of plants and animals, all perfectly adapted to the special conditions in which they live.

ICE AND SEA

Few animals could survive in an ice-covered environment but one exception is the polar bear, to many people the symbol of Arctic wildlife. With its dense fur coat and furry-soled feet, the polar bear is perfectly adapted to life on the cold, slippery ice. Polar bears are carnivores and feed on seals, which they hunt through holes in the ice or as the seals bask on the ice.

Sea mammals are particularly abundant in Arctic waters. As well as seals, there are walruses, whales and sea otters. These animals have fur or blubber, or both, to keep them warm in the icy sea. The seas provide plenty of food for these mammals, including shellfish, fish and shrimps.

Each spring, the icy Arctic seas are warmed by the sun and this slight change in temperature, probably imperceptible to people, triggers an explosion of life. Fish spawn, and crabs, shrimps and shellfish reproduce. The water teems with tiny animals called the zooplankton. Tiny ocean plants called algae also grow at the same time. The mass of zooplankton and 'blooms' of algae are food for larger creatures, forming the vital first link in the many Arctic food chains.

A polar bear's large padded feet allow it to grip as it runs across the ice. Its thick fur provides protection from the cold, even allowing it to swim in the cold Arctic seas.

In summer, the tundra provides rich grazing for migrating caribou or reindeer herds.

The abundance of fish and small sea creatures attracts millions of seabirds to the Arctic each spring to breed. There are wading birds, gulls, geese and ducks of many species. One sea bird, the Arctic tern, is truly a long-distance champion. It arrives in spring to breed in the Arctic and in the autumn flies to the Antarctic, at the other end of the world, where summer is just beginning.

THE TUNDRA

The tundra stretches from the Arctic coastline south to the forest fringing the Arctic Circle. Its peaty soil supports many kinds of acid-loving heath plants, such as bilberry, cranberry and heather-like shrubs, as well as grasses, lichens and mosses. The fierce, cold winds that howl across the tundra prevent plants from growing tall and the willow, birch and pine trees that are to be found here are all miniature versions of the full-size trees that grow in warmer climates.

All Arctic plants are adapted to their cold environment, many having rosettes of leaves and a hairy covering to keep them warm. When buried under a layer of winter snow, they are protected from their worst enemy – bitingly cold frosts. Under the snow blanket, the temperature is warmer than the freezing air above.

The Arctic growing season is very short, with just three months of good daylight and warmer temperatures. The plants must quickly take advantage of these favourable conditions and so when the temperature rises, the tundra bursts into flower, suddenly becoming a mass of colourful blooms and grasses. As the plants produce berries, they provide a valuable food source for the many small mammals, birds and insects that live on the tundra.

▲
Terns feed in the Arctic during the summer in areas such as this wetland in Iceland.

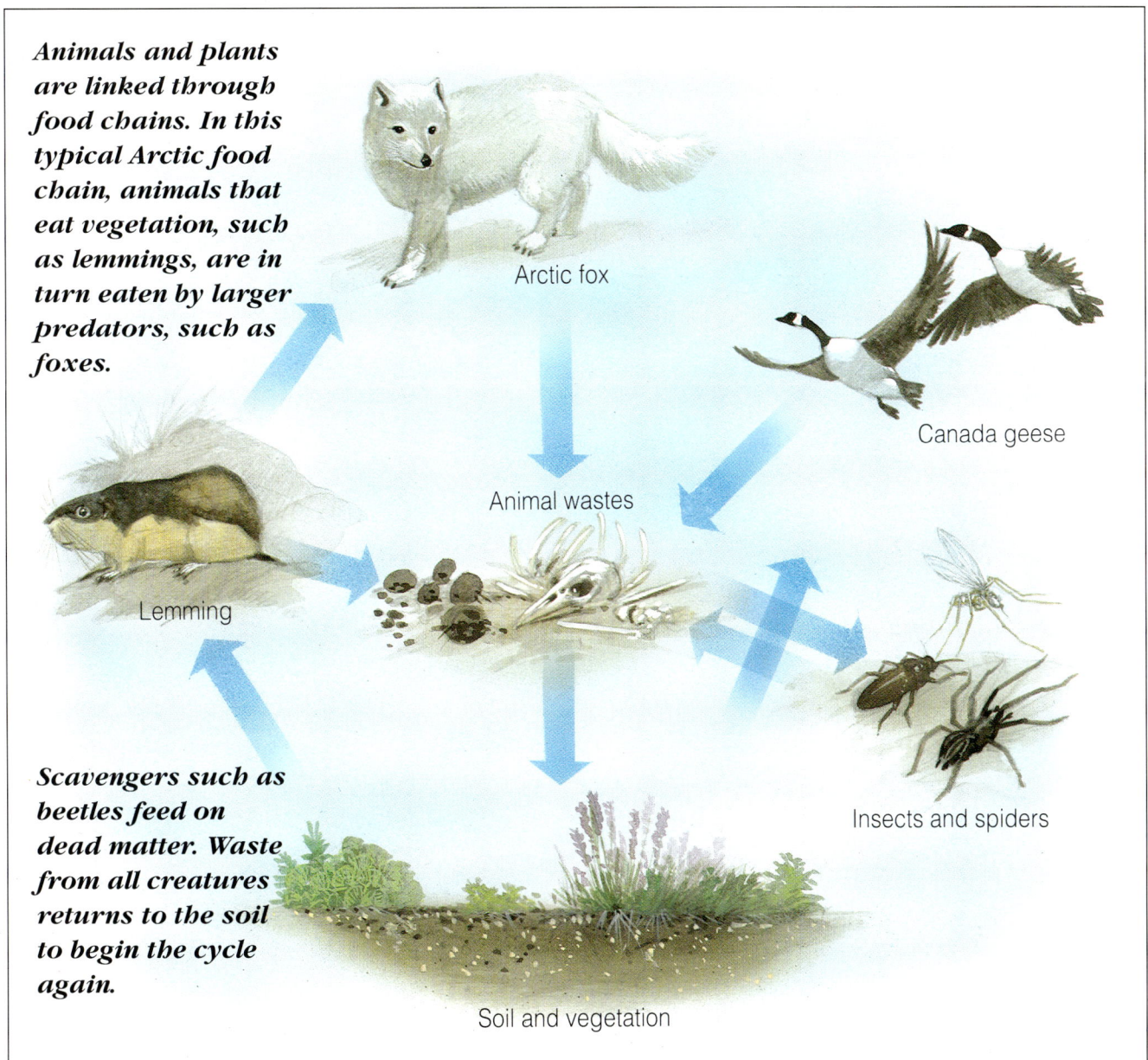

Animals and plants are linked through food chains. In this typical Arctic food chain, animals that eat vegetation, such as lemmings, are in turn eaten by larger predators, such as foxes.

Arctic fox

Canada geese

Animal wastes

Lemming

Insects and spiders

Scavengers such as beetles feed on dead matter. Waste from all creatures returns to the soil to begin the cycle again.

Soil and vegetation

As well as small herbivores, like lemmings, hares and voles, larger mammals live in the tundra. These include musk oxen and the large deer called caribou (in North America) or reindeer (in Europe and Asia). The small tundra mammals are preyed on by the Arctic fox, ermine and wolverine. The grey wolf and grizzly bear are also occasional tundra hunters and mainly kill caribou. Caribou make a long northward migration between their wintering grounds in the south and their summer calving grounds, on the northern tundra. Four species of birds spend the whole year on the high tundra: the snowy owl, the gyrfalcon, the raven and the ptarmigan. During the long winter, ptarmigan survive by eating willow twigs and buds. However, the ptarmigan themselves are the prey of the snowy owl and gyrfalcon.

With its surprisingly rich and varied wildlife, the tundra is a very special habitat. Even in the depths of winter, it is far from the wilderness it might appear to be.

▲
The raven's cleverness and resourcefulness at finding food have made it a central character in many Inuit stories.

◄

Brown bears, called grizzlies in North America, eat all kinds of food and are even skilled at catching river fish such as salmon.

In southern Siberia, the edge of the taiga forest merges with more open land.

THE TAIGA

At the edge of the Arctic Circle, there is a band of dense forest called the taiga. This forms the border of the Arctic region, gradually overlapping with the tundra further north. Generally, the taiga is a forest of conifers, such as spruce, pine and larch. Conifers are adapted to survive colder climates, having small, waxy, needle-like leaves that can withstand the icy blasts of drying winds. The larch is an exception; it sheds its more delicate needles for the winter.

The taiga is a permanent home to many animals. Squirrels and small birds feed on the cones, berries and seeds. Caribou and moose seek shelter here, especially in winter. There are also large predators, such as wolves, brown bears, and lynx, plus smaller carnivores, such as martens and stoats.

Perhaps you are surprised by the variety of plants and animals that live within the Arctic region. They can only survive by adapting their lives to fit in with the conditions imposed by the climate and the seasonal cycles. Plants, insects, birds and mammals fine-tune their feeding and breeding to make the most of what the Arctic offers them.

· T H E · A R C T I C · H O M E L A N D ·

Saami in northern Norway make a living from their reindeer herds.

The Arctic was first settled thousands of years ago. It became home to many different peoples, each with its own traditions and way of life.

The best known people are the Inuit, or Eskimos. They are the most northerly people of the Arctic, and inhabit the icy coasts of Greenland, Canada and Alaska. It is thought they first reached the Arctic from Mongolian Asia, about 10,000 years ago. Traditionally, they hunt fish, birds, seals, walruses and whales. These animals provide the Inuit with all their needs –

food, oil for staying warm and for cooking, clothing and skins for making tents and boats, and teeth and bones for making tools.

One small group of Arctic people inhabits a chain of islands and so their lives are based around the sea. The people are called the Aleut, and are related to the Inuit. They have a population of just 10,000. Their home is the Aleutian Islands, which lie in the Bering Sea, off the coast of Alaska. Like the Inuit, in the past they have depended on fish and sea mammals for survival.

The other Arctic peoples generally live further south, where the tundra merges with the trees of the northern forests. Lapland is a large area of tundra and forest, spanning northern Norway, Sweden, Finland, and northwest Russia. The original settlers of this area were a Nordic people called Saami or Lapps. Traditionally, they lived as nomads, following the herds of caribou that migrated across the tundra. The Saami relied on the caribou for meat, milk and skins for clothing. Today some 40–50,000 traditional Saami survive.

▲
At a Saami wedding, guests wear their traditional dress.

Arctic Homelands

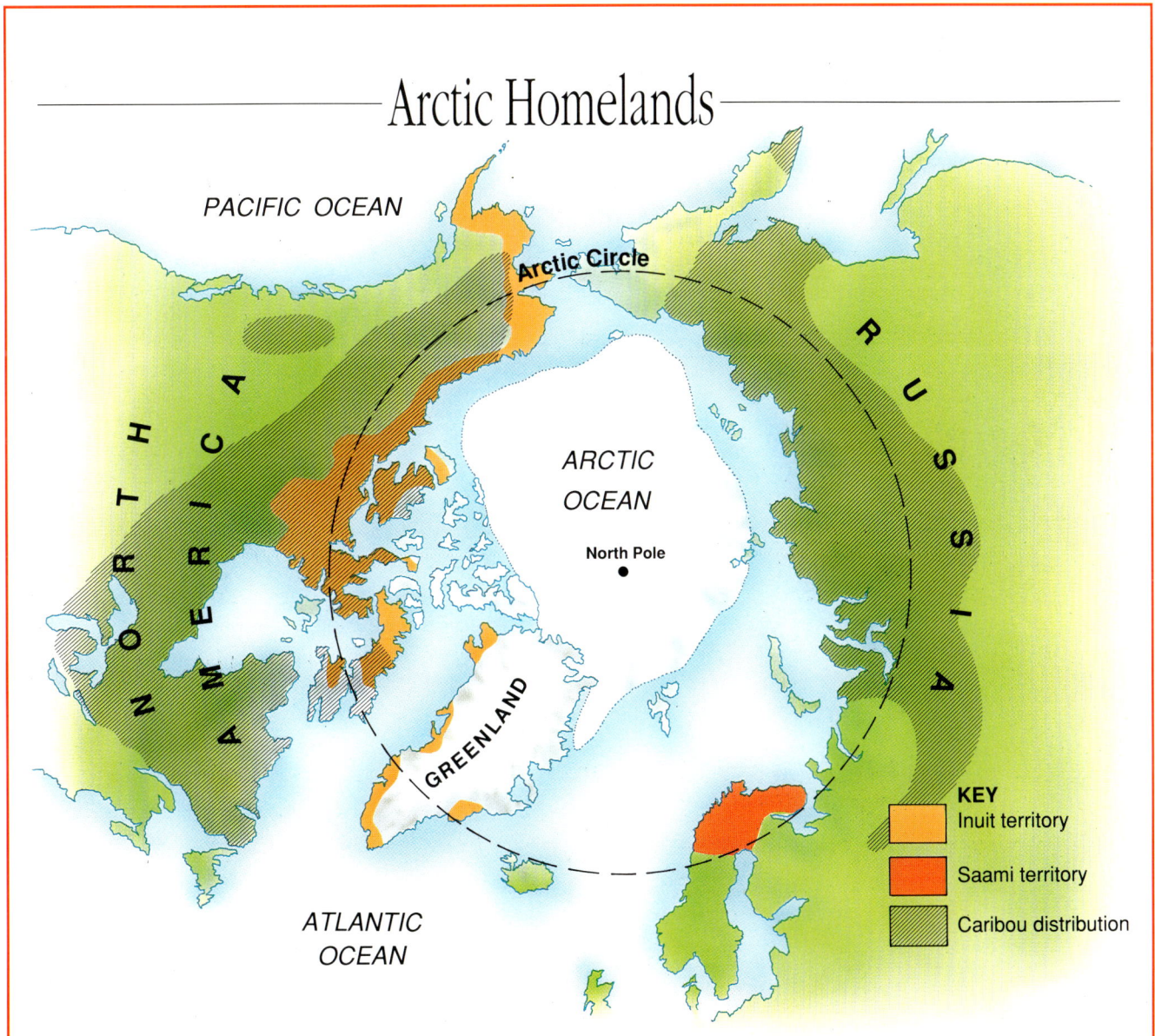

PACIFIC OCEAN

Arctic Circle

ARCTIC OCEAN

North Pole

NORTH AMERICA

RUSSIA

GREENLAND

ATLANTIC OCEAN

KEY
Inuit territory
Saami territory
Caribou distribution

ARCTIC RESOURCES

Caribou are important to many traditional peoples of the Arctic. In remote forest areas, people depend on them just as the Inuit depend on sea mammals. The Athabascan Indians or Dene probably reached Arctic North America by following caribou (reindeer) on their migrations. Originally these people came from northern Asia. Caribou herding is also traditional among the Naskapi people of northeast Canada, and the Nentsy and Evenki peoples of Arctic Russia.

All of these people have successfully made their home in the Arctic, but only by finding ingenious ways of using the natural resources available, especially the mammals and fish. Without these resources, no people could have survived in the harsh Arctic environment.

It is important to remember that these Arctic peoples had quite small populations, and they traditionally lived scattered over a very large area. These small groups of people could easily be supported by the numbers of fish and mammals living in the Arctic. Because they took only what they needed to survive, the Arctic peoples rarely disturbed the natural balance of their environment.

However, the traditional lifestyle of the Arctic peoples is disappearing, and new settlers have arrived in the region. Instead of living in the traditional way using natural resources just to keep alive, the newcomers want to use the Arctic's resources for profit. This can mean taking more from the environment than it can stand. You can read about the consequences of this in the next chapter.

Hunting is still an important activity in parts of the Arctic. These Canadian Inuit use both dogs and snow scooters when they hunt across the vast icy wastes.

▲
An igloo is a temporary hunter's shelter built from slabs of snow and ice.

THE INUIT LIFESTYLE

For thousands of years, the Inuit have lived successfully on the inhospitable coasts of Greenland, Canada and Alaska. They can find all they need to survive in the natural world around them. Traditional Inuit clothing is made from the skins of animals such as caribou, polar bear, seals and Arctic fox, as well as the feathers of birds. Such furs keep the animals warm, and so the Inuit use them for the same purpose.

The traditional Inuit have a meat-based diet, centred around seals, whales, walrus and caribou. In winter especially, the Inuit spear seals and walrus through holes in the ice. In the summer some hunt caribou on the tundra and others catch fish and whales in the sea. Traditionally, the Inuit used carved bone spears and bows and arrows as hunting weapons, until settlers brought guns to the Arctic. Seal meat is the most important meat to most Inuit. This shows in the Inuit name for seals, which means giver of life. In summer, the Inuit vary their diet with berries and birds' eggs gathered from the tundra.

Nowadays, many Inuit live in houses, but in the past they used various kinds of homes, depending on the season. In winter they built huts of rock and turf or made snow-block igloos when away from home on long hunting trips. In summer, their homes were tents made of seal or caribou skin, stretched over a wooden or bone framework. Blubber lamps made these homes warm and cosy inside.

For transport, the Inuit used wooden sledges, sometimes drawn by dogs. On the water, they used boats made from a wooden or bone framework covered in sealskin. The kayak is a small, slender canoe which an Inuit hunter uses to glide through the water to hunt seals or fish. The kumiak is a larger boat, used by Inuit teams for hunting whales. Now most people use skidoos and motor boats to travel.

Inuit traditionally live in close family units and have a society based on equality and sharing. In the past, especially, the peaceful Inuit people believed in spirits, such as Sila, the great force that controls and oversees everything the people do. Since the arrival of settlers from North America and parts of Europe, the Christian religion has influenced Inuit beliefs although in some places traditional religion is becoming more popular.

Inuit Handicrafts

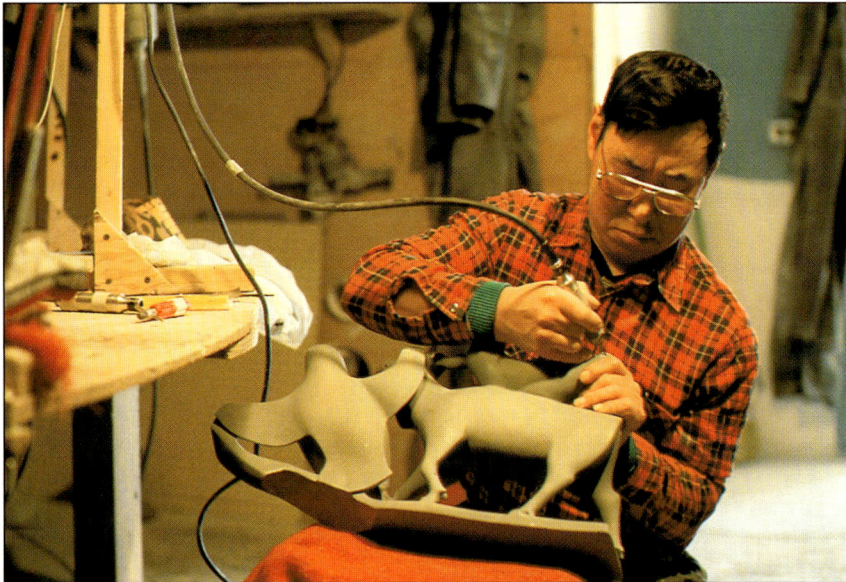

This Canadian Inuit craftsman is using an electric drill to carve a figure in soapstone, which he can later sell.

The Inuit are skilled people in all they do – hunting, building homes and boats, and making clothes. From natural materials such as bone and skin, they could make a great range of tools and objects. Bone could be used for needles, spears, fish barbs, and hunting sticks. Ivory from whale and walrus teeth was used to make beautiful carvings of humans and animals, and delicate charm bracelets. Caribou leather can be used to make beautifully patterned, soft play-balls for children.

· EARLY · TRADING ·

*E*xpeditions by Europeans to find sea routes around the Arctic ice to the Pacific Ocean began in the sixteenth century, but without success. Until about 200 years ago, the Arctic peoples carried on their traditional way of life with little contact with other people. This changed when newcomers began to settle in the northern lands in search of wealth.

In 1741, a Russian ship *St Peter*, commanded by Vitus Bering, set sail from Siberia. Eventually, the ship passed the Aleutian Islands and reached the coast of what is now Alaska. This opened up Arctic America and soon many Europeans were arriving to explore this new land of opportunity. They found animals that were new to them, such as sea otters, and realized that they could make a profitable trade from their soft fur. At about the same time in Siberia, Russian explorers were trapping small mammals, such as mink. And so the Arctic fur trade began. By the early part of the twentieth century, it had greatly reduced the populations of mammals such as sea otters.

An old engraving of a whale in Melville Bay, Canada, shows the danger faced by early whalers in their small, open boats.

Exploiting Arctic Resources

Three sperm whales look small when seen from the deck of the modern whaler that has just killed them.

The new visitors to the Arctic were very interested in the many whales they saw in Arctic seas. Whale oil could be used in lamps and to make soaps, while baleen from the whale's mouth was in demand for ladies' corsets. Soon a huge international trade in whale products was flourishing. Thousands of northern right whales were slaughtered. By the late 1800s, they had almost been wiped out.

From a population of about 30,000 their numbers had fallen to just a few hundred.

The examples of the whaling and fur trades show that new visitors to the Arctic viewed the region's native mammals as a profitable resource. By contrast, the traditional Arctic peoples had used whales and seals as a means of survival. If you object to the idea of killing animals, you may feel that hunting

them for any reason is wrong. But there is an important difference between using the environment for survival and using it for profit. There is also a difference between taking from the environment in moderation and taking in excess. These differences highlight a key issue facing the Arctic: should the region be kept unchanged or should its natural resources be exploited?

THE GREAT GOLD RUSH

The Arctic has other natural resources besides its great wealth of animal life. One of the most famous resources is gold. In the 1880s, gold-hunters came by the thousands to Arctic America, seeking their fortunes. The news had spread that valuable nuggets of gold had been found in the Yukon river in Alaska. During this stampede for gold, the newcomers built cottages and cabins in remote parts of the country and by 1900 large settlements had sprung up. The great gold rush changed the face of Alaska completely.

By the early part of this century, much of the remote Arctic had been opened up. The fur trade, whaling and events such as the gold rush brought many new settlers to the region from Europe and further south in the USA. As the new settlers arrived, they brought with them a lifestyle very different from that of the traditional Arctic peoples. The new settlers set up homes, shops, schools and Christian churches. As the original Arctic peoples came into contact with the outsiders, their world changed forever.

In the 1880s, gold prospectors rushed to the Yukon to make their fortunes.

▶ *In Iqaluit, a small town in Frobisher Bay, Canada, Inuit children enjoy all the benefits of modern school buildings and facilities.*

◀ *An Inuit couple discuss a purchase at the well-stocked Hudson Bay store, in Canada's Northwest Territory. Unemployment leaves most Inuit with little spare money for buying luxury goods.*

A NEW WAY OF LIFE

When the first explorers arrived, some treated the original peoples harshly. Many Inuit died because they had no natural immunity to the new diseases brought by the settlers. Even a minor illness like measles could kill people. The Europeans and Americans introduced new foods, such as sugar, and alcohol. These affected the health of some Inuit, who were not used to them. As the settlers mixed with the original peoples, there were conflicts over land, language, religion and culture. Usually it was the Inuit who came off worst in these encounters.

Over time, the traditional peoples and new settlers have had to come to terms with sharing the Arctic, and today the different groups of people live alongside one another. Some groups of the original peoples carry on their traditional and unique lifestyle, living simply in the natural environment. But most have begun to live a more Western way of life. For example, the US and Canadian Inuit now speak English and tend to use motorized snow-mobiles, rather than traditional sledges. Instead of living in igloos, the Inuit usually live in modern homes, with video recorders, televisions and computers.

As in many other parts of the world, there are towns in the Arctic with modern supermarkets, health centres, schools and takeaways. Some of the towns have a high population of Inuit or Saami peoples. In Alaska and Siberia there are new industrial towns. Murmansk is an important Siberian centre for engineering, chemicals and military industries. In contrast, there is Tromsø, a bustling Norwegian fishing port located just below 70°N. It is the world's most northerly city.

▲
Arctic ports such as Tromsø in Norway are increasingly popular tourist destinations.

NEW INDUSTRIES

In the past, the Arctic peoples survived by living simply, using the natural resources around them. Today most people who live in the Arctic are there to work for money, rather than simply trying to survive in the natural environment. Life is often based on traditional Arctic resources: sea mammals, fish, reindeer and the sub-arctic forests, but the modern approach has turned these resources into industries: meat production, skin and fur processing, fishing and forestry.

▲
Russian gold miners in Magadan, in eastern Siberia.

▲
Today, Saami often use modern forms of transport to help with traditional activities.

CHANGING LIFESTYLES

Today most Saami lead a very different lifestyle from their traditional life as nomads, following reindeer (caribou) herds. Now most Saami are not involved with herding reindeer at all. Those who do keep reindeer are mostly farmers, rather than herders. They make money by selling the meat from their reindeer, and some Saami are very wealthy because of this. For example, they can afford expensive helicopters, which they use to round up the reindeer.

The Saami people are still proud of their culture and traditions and occasionally wear their beautiful traditional costumes. But sometimes this is more for the benefit of fascinated tourists than to keep warm. Today, Saami are involved in many industries, especially mining, fishing and forestry, which are described later in this chapter.

Canadian sealers hunt seal pups for their skins.

The Inuit lifestyle has also changed a great deal. Traditionally, the Inuit lived by harvesting the sea mammals around them for food and clothing. But, as the international demand for sealskins increased, the Inuit were under pressure to earn a living by hunting seals and selling their skins. From the 1960s to the 1980s, an enormous number of seals were killed in the Canadian Arctic to satisfy the demand for soft seal pup fur in Europe and North America. In particular, the white fur of harp seal pups and blue-grey fur of hooded seal pups was in demand. The slaughter was on a massive scale: in 1982, 167,000 harp seal pelts were taken in Canada.

This trade in seal fur outraged conservationists and, as a result, the European Community banned the trade in sealskin products. This led to the collapse of the seal fur market, which also brought about financial disaster for the Arctic seal hunters.

Today the Inuit still hunt seals for meat and clothing but on a much smaller scale than during the peak of the seal fur trade. The total number of pelts taken is a few thousand, and many people think that seal populations can withstand this level of hunting. The Inuit use every part of the seals they hunt – meat, bones, fur – but now, due to the collapse of the fur market, they cannot get a good price for the skins and find it hard to carry on this activity. To make a living, some Inuit have turned to fishing and some have also begun to herd caribou.

FISHING

Today fishing is a very important part of the lifestyle of Arctic people. While in the past Arctic peoples caught fish to meet their own needs, today fishing is a major business and thousands of people depend on it for their livelihood. In Alaska, fishing provides more jobs than any other industry. There are still Dene and Inuit who catch fish in small quantities to meet the needs of their small communities. But generally, fishing in the Arctic is now conducted on a very large scale using the latest technology.

A few kinds of fish are crucial to the Arctic economy. They include salmon, which live in rivers, and cod, which live in the cold Arctic seas. The cod are fished by fleets from many nations. As well as being fished, salmon can also be farmed. In addition, crabs and king prawns are widely caught, especially in Alaska, Greenland and Norway.

However, the large-scale fishing operations in the Arctic put Arctic fish stocks under threat. Overfishing has already caused a sharp decline in the numbers of herring, once a common fish. To reduce the chances of this catastrophe occurring again with other kinds of fish, it is vital that the number of fish caught is strictly controlled.

Fortunately, there are now international fishing quotas, designed to protect fish populations. These control how many fish can be caught each year by fishing nations. There are also rules concerning the size of mesh used in fishing nets. The mesh may not be smaller than a legal minimum size, which allows young fish to slip through the net and breed. This control is designed to allow fish populations to remain steady, to the benefit of all, including the many animals that rely on fish for their survival.

Fishing is vital to the economy of many nations and there are often disputes over who has the right to fish in certain areas. Despite the quotas some traditional Arctic people, like the Inuit, feel that their own fishing rights are threatened by the huge fishing fleets that have moved into Arctic seas.

Arctic seas are rich fishing grounds. Factory ships freeze and process the catches brought to them by fleets of trawlers. Too much fishing has already caused the numbers of herring to decline.

FORESTRY

The taiga – the conifer forest at the edge of the Arctic region – is another important resource. Traditionally, Arctic peoples such as the Saami cut trees as they needed them, mostly for firewood. Today, however, forestry is a major industry in Arctic Russia, Sweden and Finland. The governments of these countries give financial support to forestry because it provides much-needed employment in remote Arctic areas.

Controlled forestry does not harm the environment permanently, because it encourages new trees to grow – they are a renewable natural resource. But in Russia, especially, there is strong economic pressure to harvest too many trees. Every year, 3 million hectares are cut from the taiga but not enough of these trees are being replaced. The slow-growing northern forests cannot support this level of timber extraction for ever.

As well as allowing the trees to regrow, it is important to allow some forest areas to remain undisturbed, so that the wildlife that lives there does not suffer. Like the other resources of the Arctic, timber must be managed carefully so that the environment does not suffer from over-exploitation.

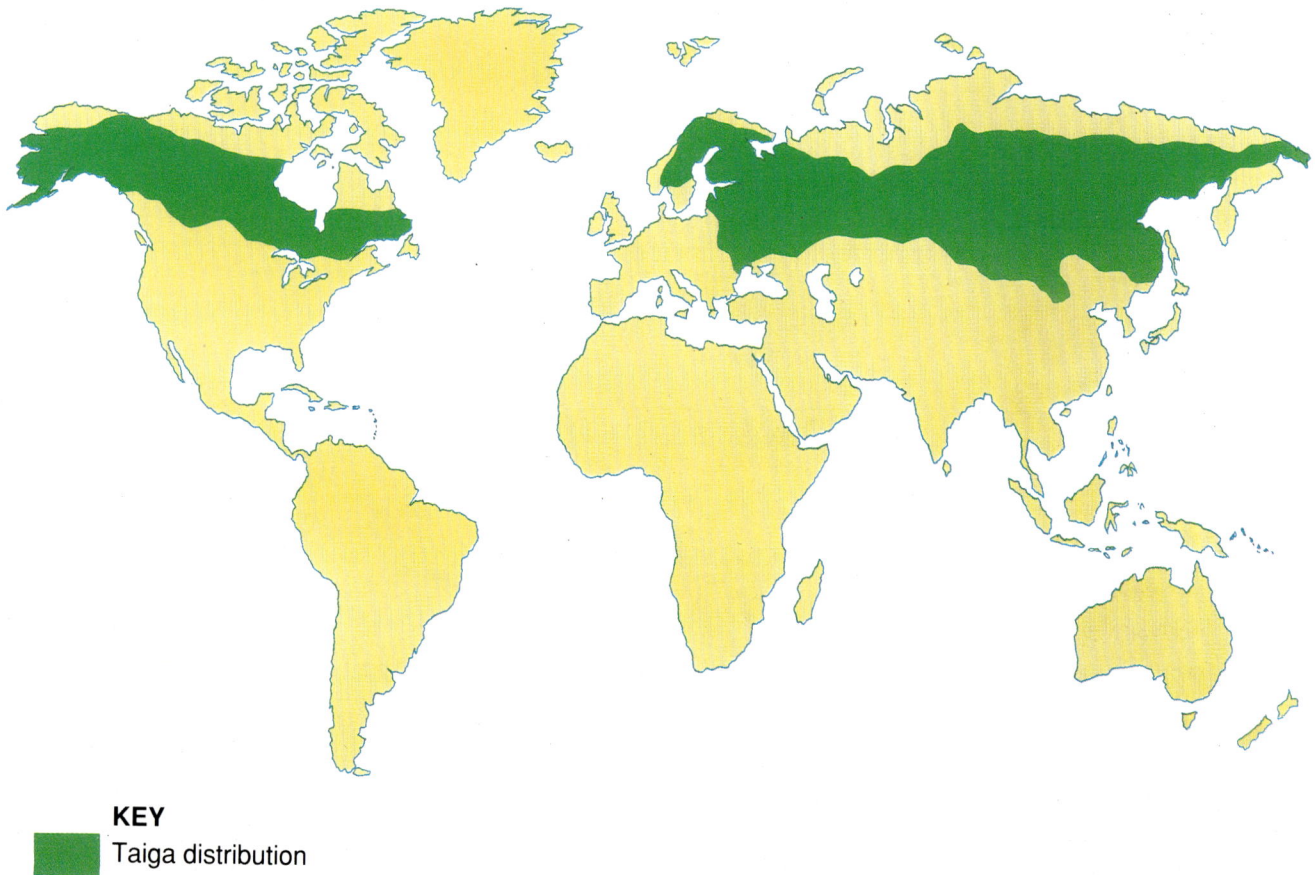

KEY

Taiga distribution

▲
The taiga forests stretch in a band across the northern hemisphere..

Arctic Beauty

▲
A bright growth of yellow marsh saxifrage fringes a stream in the Arctic landscape.

A Russian's view of Arctic beauty:
'We are proud, not only of the yield of timber, but of our majestic-looking forests and picturesque meadows. We love our silvery birch groves . . . (and) fir and spruce . . . And those of us who find ourselves in the tundra in spring enjoy the coloured carpet of flowers . . . The proximity of animals and bird life enriches our own, bringing us joy and beauty. All of this reminds us of the need to keep the productivity of wildlife at a high level, whether or not it is used directly for man's good, and of the need to protect life on earth in all its forms.'
S. V. Kalesnik &
V. F. Pavlenko
*Soviet Union: A
Geographical Survey,*
1976

· D E V E L O P I N G · T H E · A R C T I C ·

Mammals, forests and fish are three important natural resources of the Arctic. But the region's mineral resources are more valuable to developers. The Arctic has a wealth of metals, such as copper, iron ore, lead, zinc and nickel. Precious gold, platinum and diamonds are found in Alaska and Siberia. There is also a plentiful supply of the fossil fuels: coal, oil and gas.

These fuels and metals are in demand for international markets, and so can bring much-needed income to the countries in the Arctic. The extraction of metals and fuels provides employment for people in remote Arctic areas, and attracts outside workers into the region. For these reasons, the governments of the various Arctic countries are keen to develop their mineral resources.

An Alaskan oil rig. Parts of the Arctic are rich in mineral resources, such as oil, but the living conditions of workers there can be harsh.

Inuit children help unload the helicopter that brings supplies to Savissivik in remote northwest Greenland.

THE COST OF DEVELOPMENT

Although mineral extraction brings wealth to the Arctic, it is a costly business. Developing the Arctic minerals industry is not straightforward. Transport networks have to be constructed to link remote Arctic mines or fuel deposits to the main industrial centres of the countries that own them. This is expensive and complicated. The Arctic climate, with its snowdrifts, fogs and permafrost, is a major obstacle to mineral extraction. Then there are the problems of looking after the people who come to work in the remote mines or oilfields. Where will they live, and where will their food come from? The harsh Arctic climate is not suited to growing crops or keeping farm livestock, and so a lot of food has to be brought in from outside the region.

There is another cost of mineral extraction – the cost to the environment. Digging out minerals or drilling for oil and gas inevitably disturbs the natural habitat. As well as creating the site itself, roads and railways must be built and pipelines laid. During this process the fragile tundra soil can easily be damaged, and the habitats of rare plants and animals destroyed. The mining process can pollute groundwater and rivers. For example, gold mining has polluted the water in some areas of Alaska. Air pollution can arise from the smelting of metals and this has happened in the Russian Arctic.

Throughout the Arctic, there are conflicts between those who wish to develop the region's mineral wealth and those who want to protect the environment. A well-known conflict surrounds the oil extraction business in Alaska.

▲
Pollution from mines such as this one threatens the ecological balance of the region.

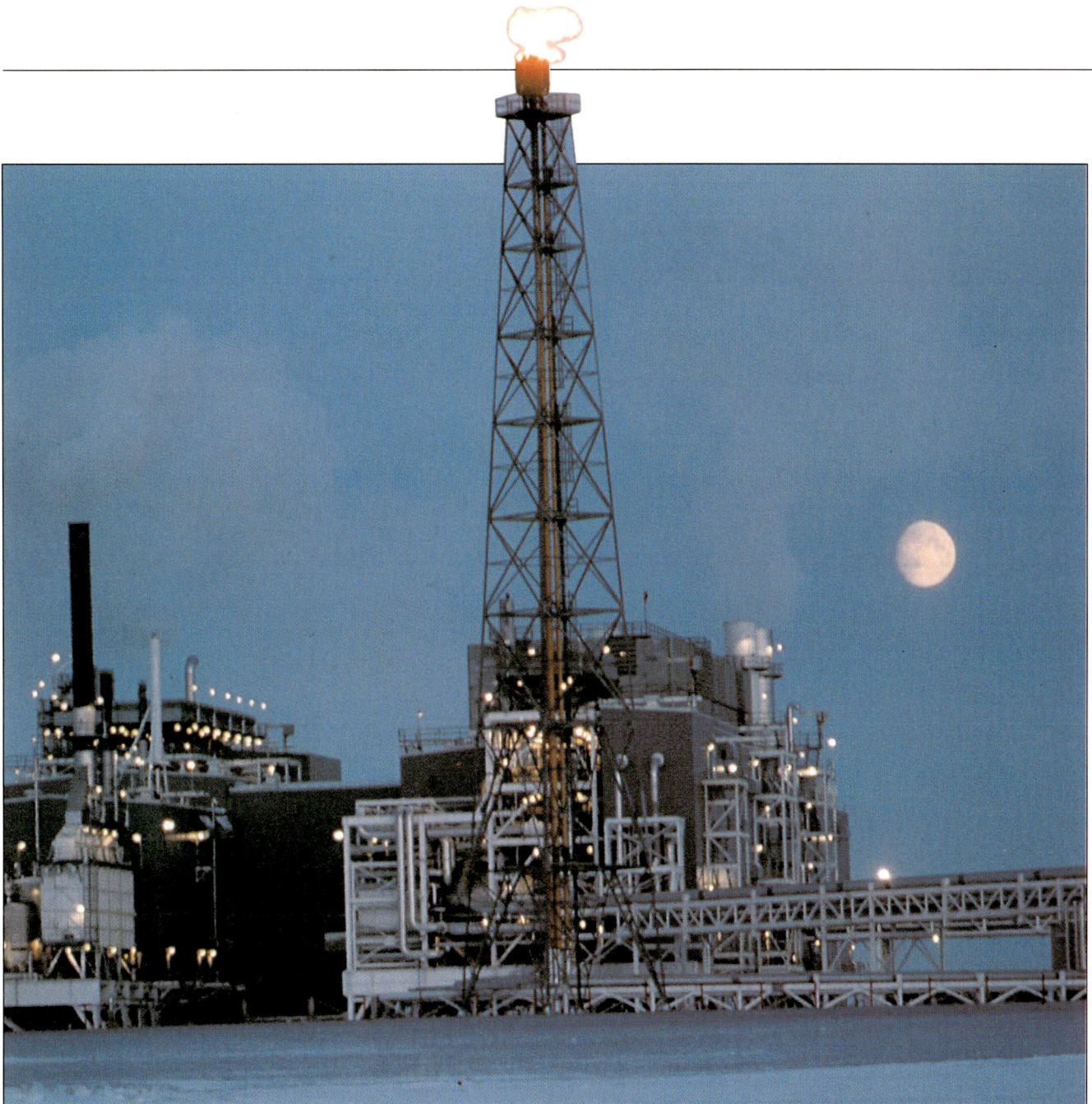

▲
An oil rig at Endicott Island, Prudhoe Bay in Alaska.

ALASKA'S 'BLACK GOLD'

In 1968, an enormous oilfield was discovered at Prudhoe Bay and oil companies were keen to develop it. There was strong opposition from conservationists and the Athabascan and Inuit peoples. As a result, the government set aside a large area – called the Arctic National Wildlife Reserve (ANWR) – for the traditional peoples and the animals of the area, and paid a billion dollars to be divided between the people. However, oil companies are now campaigning to be allowed to drill for oil on the ANWR, which would disrupt the lives of the caribou herds that calve there.

▲ ▶

The Arctic pipeline starts in Prudhoe Bay (inset) then cuts its course through miles of unspoilt country (right) on its way to the port of Valdez, where the oil is loaded on to tankers.

Between 1974 and 1977, the Trans-Alaska Pipeline was built to connect the Prudhoe Bay oilfield with Valdez, a port on the south coast of Alaska. The pipeline stretches 1,300 km, crossing tundra, forest and mountains. During its construction, the developers tried to avoid disrupting special wildlife sites and the migration routes of caribou. When the oil began to flow, it boosted Alaska's economy and now accounts for 87 per cent of the gross state product. Developing the oilfield

has brought wealth to Alaska and has generated work for many people. But in 1989, the catastrophic *Exxon Valdez* oil spill occurred, which increased people's concerns over the Alaskan oil industry.

By early next century, the Prudhoe Bay oil reserve will have been exhausted and developers will be seeking new oilfields. Some people fear that they will turn to areas of land set aside for the traditional Arctic peoples, or protected as wildlife havens.

USING WATER POWER

With so many rivers in the Arctic, hydroelectric power (HEP) seems an ideal way to make electricity. Harnessing water power to create energy does not cause pollution, unlike burning fossil fuels. However, HEP schemes do involve damming rivers and creating large reservoirs.

At present the Cree and Inuit people of northern Quebec in Canada are concerned about the second phase of the James Bay hydroelectricity scheme. The project began in 1973, when three major rivers were diverted, flooding a huge area of land, poisoning rivers and drowning hunting grounds. If the second phase begins in 1993, twenty rivers will be diverted, affecting an area the size of France.

The Canadian government supports the scheme, believing it will provide much-needed electricity and create jobs. But the local people claim the scheme will cause an environmental disaster. Plans to build a dam across the Great Whale River would badly affect the traditional way of life of the Cree and Inuit.

La Grande (shown here) is just one of the rivers affected by the dams of the James Bay hydroelectricity scheme.

At present, they use the river for drinking water, fishing and transport. But if the river were dammed, its flow would be drastically reduced. Environmental groups, such as Greenpeace, warn that this could upset the natural saltwater balance in the coastal water of James Bay. Then the spring blooms of algae and plankton might be affected, which would damage the whole ecosystem. This conflict illustrates the dilemma over how the Arctic's natural resources should be used.

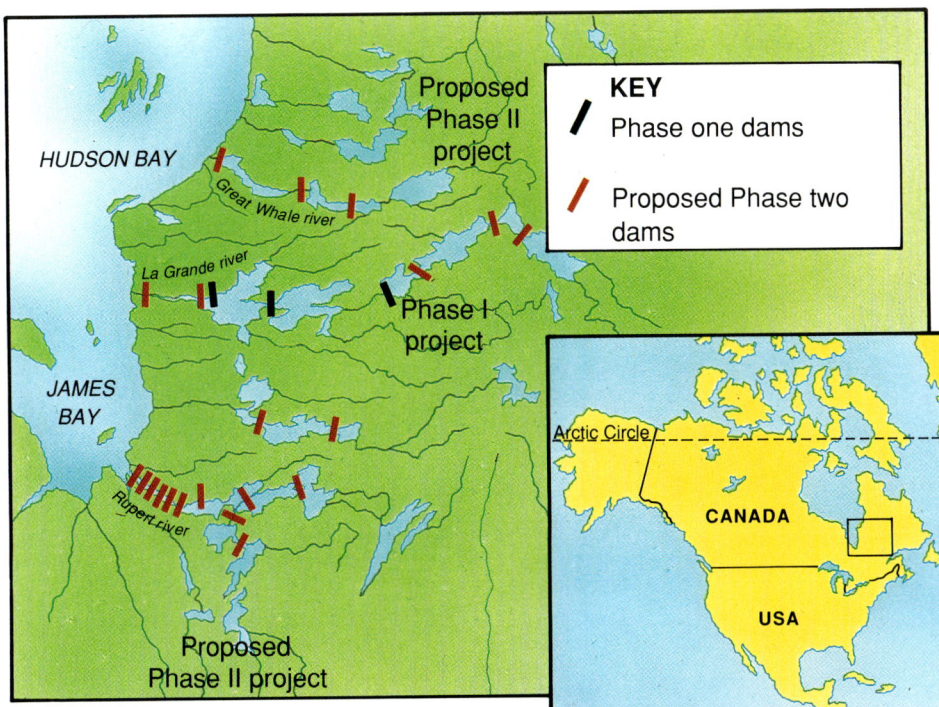

This map shows the James Bay hydroelectricity scheme. The black lines mark the dams built in 1973. The red lines show the large number of new dams proposed for the second phase of the project, which is due to start in 1993.

Case study: The *Exxon Valdez* disaster

On 23 March 1989, the oil tanker *Exxon Valdez* was passing through Prince William Sound in the Gulf of Alaska, laden with a cargo of crude oil from Prudhoe Bay. Suddenly, the vessel hit a rocky reef, making an enormous hole in its side. The tanker began to leak oil but it was many hours before emergency teams arrived to deal with the problem. By that time, millions of gallons of oil had spread out over the offshore water. Local people and emergency teams tried to contain the spill, using booms and skimmers, but the damage had been done.

U S A

ALASKA

Valdez

Bligh reef

Prince William Sound

Oil slick

Orca Bay

Cordova

Seward

Montague Island

GULF OF ALASKA

This map shows the extent of the oil slick from the wreck of the **Exxon Valdez.**

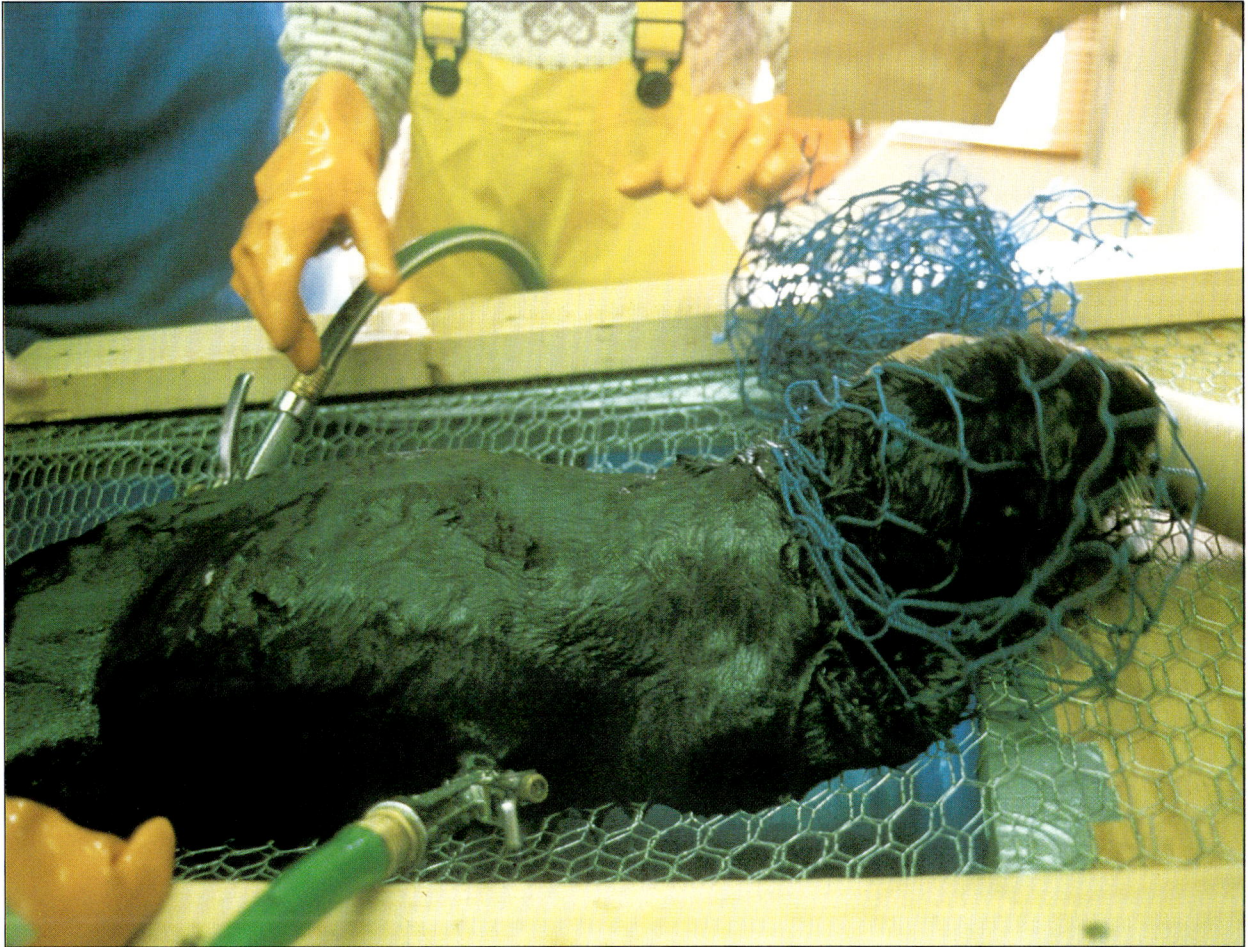

▲
This sea otter was lucky to be rescued from the oil slick around the **Exxon Valdez.**

The effects were devastating. A thick, black sludge covered the shores of Prince William Sound and clogged the fur and feathers of the area's wildlife. Within a week of the spill, rescue workers had counted the first casualties: 24,000 dead seabirds and 1,000 sea otters. The oil spill also harmed many other kinds of marine life, from shrimps to salmon. The effects were passed on up the food chain to the area's brown bears.

In the following months, the Exxon company funded the clean-up of the oil-covered beaches. But the impact of the disaster was immense: apart from the toll of dead animals, it had also damaged the livelihood of local fishermen. The region around Kodiak Island was especially badly hit, and this is the USA's third largest fish producing area. Although most signs of the spill have disappeared, its impact on the environment and local people will be long-lasting.

So far, we have looked at the pressures on the Arctic as its resources are developed. This is pressure from the inside – from the Arctic countries. But the region is also affected by what goes on far beyond its boundaries. One example of this is pollution.

Pollution takes many forms. It can be smoke pouring out of factory chimneys or toxic chemicals spilled into the sea. Pollution is no respecter of boundaries – it can spread hundreds or even thousands of kilometres from the area where it was caused.

AIR POLLUTION

The Arctic is famous for its clear blue skies. But in recent years, the local people have noticed a dirty layer in the sky. This is called the Arctic Haze. It is the result of air pollution from industrial parts of Europe, the former Soviet republics and North America. All the time, waste chemicals from factories and power stations are being pumped into the air above these industrial centres. Then the airborne pollutants are carried by the wind, often northwards into Arctic skies.

ACID RAIN

Chemical pollution does not just hang in the atmosphere; it affects the air we breathe and damages the natural environment. Two gases, sulphur dioxide and nitrogen dioxide, are especially damaging. They mix with moisture in the atmosphere to form a harmful cocktail called acid rain. Normal rainwater is very slightly acid but, when polluted, it becomes more so. Over time, acid rain makes lakes become more acid, sometimes killing fish. Acid rain may also harm trees, causing them to lose their leaves and even die. Conifers are especially badly affected. They shed their needles, which is an unnatural thing for most conifers to do.

Acid rain is a particular problem in the forests of northern Norway and Sweden which stretch into the Arctic Circle. Here there are signs of damaged trees with thinning branches or an excessive number of cones – clues that they are dying. The tundra is also affected. Polluted snow stays on the ground all winter and then melts quickly in spring, releasing streams of acid water. This flows into the many bogs and lakes on the tundra and harms their delicate ecosystems. Year by year, the effects of acid rain are building up in the Arctic. But the worst case of pollution was caused by an incident that occurred in a matter of seconds.

◄

The low-lying winter sun over sea ice shows the Arctic Haze. It forms as sunlight reflects off particles of water, dust or pollution in the air.

►

Acid rain is particularly harmful to conifers, which are the most common trees in the northern forests. These damaged trees are in Canada and are an important habitat for Arctic animals.

THE CHERNOBYL DISASTER

On 25 April 1986, there was an explosion at the Chernobyl nuclear power station in the Ukraine. The result was an invisible, but highly dangerous, radioactive cloud, which was carried by the wind into Arctic Finland, Sweden and Norway. When it rained, radioactive elements were washed into the ground and then absorbed by plants, especially lichens. As the Saami's reindeer grazed on the lichens, the reindeer too became radioactive. Their meat could no longer be eaten safely by people, and so many thousands of the animals had to be slaughtered. They were buried in deep trenches, so that they would not contaminate the environment.

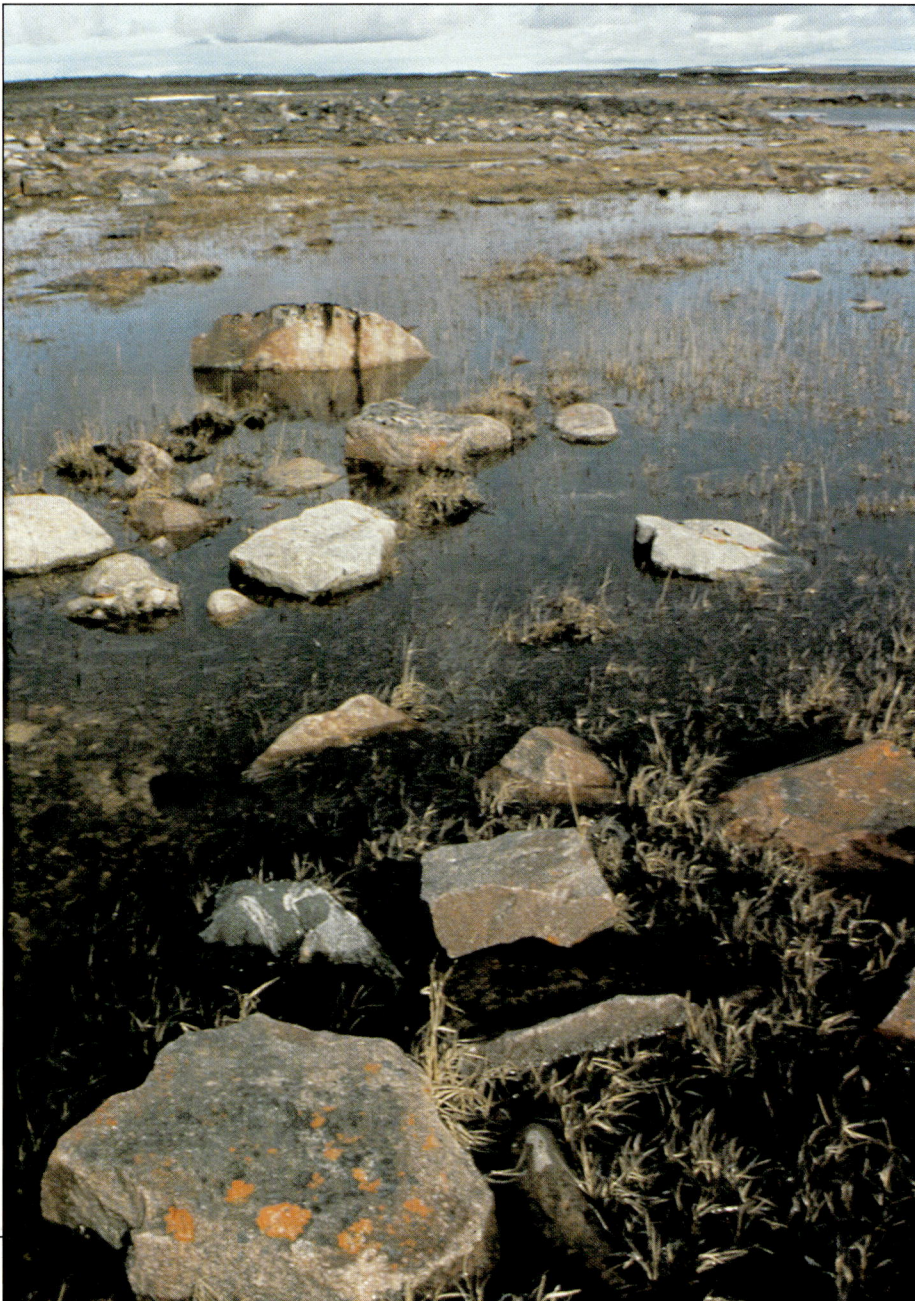

Lichens grow slowly and are vulnerable to pollution. They grow on stones and rocks and have a vital place in the ecology of the tundra. In areas affected by the explosion at Chernobyl, however, many lichens have absorbed radioactivity which makes them dangerous for animals to eat.

The reactor that exploded at the Chernobyl nuclear power station (shown here) has been sealed in concrete. The building now stands as a monument to the dangers of nuclear pollution.

The Chernobyl accident was catastrophic for the Saami reindeer herders. Moreover, it will take many years for the traces of radioactivity to disappear from the Arctic soil and plants. Of course, the disaster brought even more tragic results in the part of the Ukraine surrounding the power station. Many local people became ill following the explosion and a large area of land will be out of bounds for decades, if not longer. The strictest safety precautions are needed to prevent such a disaster happening again.

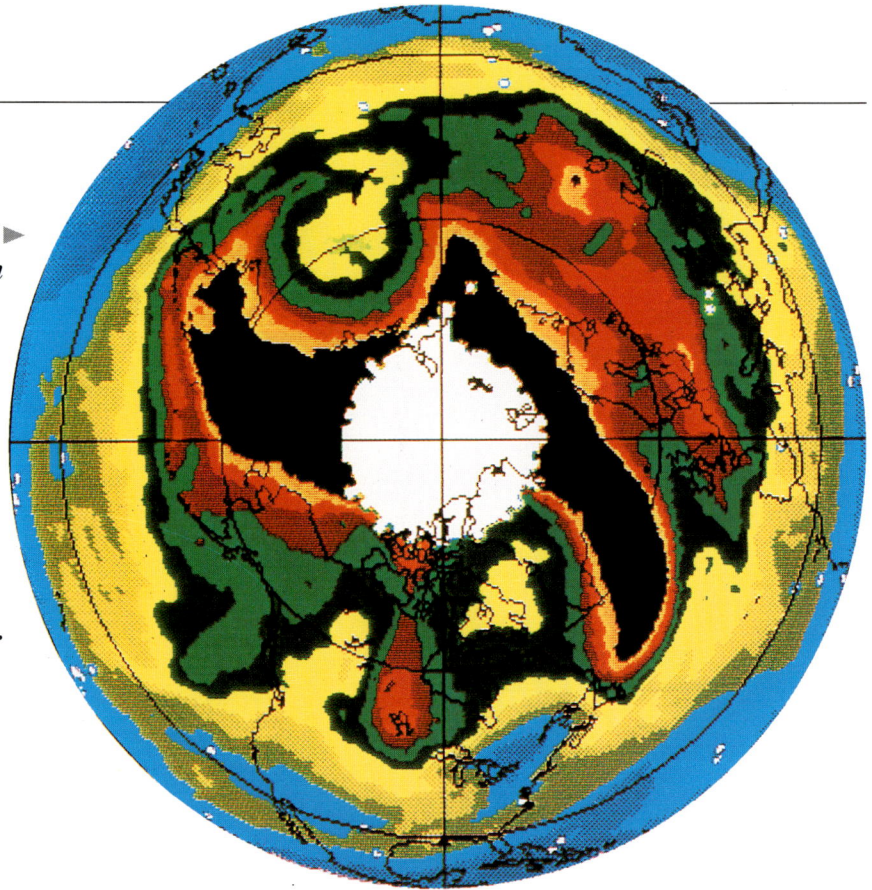

A satellite's instruments can take readings of the ozone in the atmosphere and produce a map showing different levels. This satellite map with the Arctic at the centre shows ozone levels over the northern hemisphere in February 1989. Yellow patches show low ozone levels.

OTHER THREATS

There are other environmental problems that will affect people living in the Arctic. They are caused by the everyday activities of people in all parts of the world. They are the ozone hole and the spread of harmful chemicals into the Arctic environment on the ground as well as in the air.

THE OZONE HOLE

In 1985, scientists discovered a large hole in the ozone layer of the atmosphere above Antarctica. Ozone (O_3) is a natural form of oxygen (O_2) found in the lower atmosphere, about 20 km above the earth's surface. It builds up and breaks down again in natural cycles. The ozone layer is important because it screens out the harmful ultraviolet rays from the sun. These rays are known to affect plant growth and can cause eye disorders in people, as well as skin cancer.

More recently, scientists have found that the ozone layer is disappearing in the northern hemisphere, including over the Arctic. In spring the ozone level drops to about 10 per cent below normal, but later in the year it recovers. However, the gap in the ozone layer in the northern hemisphere could be harmful to millions of people living in northern Europe and North America.

We know that the ozone is being destroyed by chlorine compounds, such as CFCs (chlorofluorocarbons) found in aerosol sprays and in the cooling mechanisms of fridges. In 1987, 24 nations signed the Montreal Protocol, an international agreement to limit the release of CFCs into the atmosphere. In June 1990, the same nations agreed to phase out the use of CFCs by the end of this century. It is now easy to find aerosols without CFCs and the race is on to develop a marketable fridge that does not contain CFCs.

Poisoned Food Chains

Toxic, or poisonous, waste is a worldwide problem – it even affects the remote Arctic. Scientists have found polar bears whose bodies contain high levels of toxic chemicals called PCBs, which are used in the electrical industry. PCBs and the pesticide DDT have been widely used in Europe and North America, but how have they reached the Arctic?

DDT can pass from crop fields into the groundwater and then enter rivers and the sea. PCBs can leak out of waste dumps or can be discharged into rivers and the sea. Ocean currents take these chemicals into Arctic waters.

Once in the environment, PCBs and DDT stay there for decades, stored in sediments or inside animals. They can then be passed through the food chain from plankton through fish to birds and sea mammals, and even to people. (See diagram.) The worst affected animals are the top predators. They eat many smaller animals with traces of toxic waste and so get huge doses of the harmful chemicals. These substances remain in the body, stored in fat. They can be found in high levels in Arctic mammals with large fat reserves, such as polar bears, seals and whales. In high doses, PCBs may cause cancer. They can also damage the nervous system and reproductive ability.

In the 1970s the use of DDT was banned in Europe and North America. The production of PCBs was banned in the USA in 1979. Where toxic waste pollution has been controlled, the wildlife is slowly recovering. But it will take many years for all the existing traces of PCBs and DDT to disappear from the Arctic.

Chemicals dumped into sea

Toxic chemicals
(such as PCBs and DDT)

Killer whales

Plankton

Fishes

Seals and other
marine mammals

Polar bears

Seabirds

· P R O T E C T I N G · T H E · A R C T I C ·

As you have seen, the Arctic is changing rapidly. The region is opening up, as more of its resources are developed. The development of the Arctic is a mixed blessing: it creates new wealth, but at the same time it changes the environment and makes it hard for the region's original peoples to live a traditional lifestyle. The way forward for the region could lie somewhere between the two extremes of over-development and total conservation.

But who will watch over the Arctic, to ensure the region is not spoiled in the future? This is a complicated matter, since eight countries have lands in the Arctic region. Each of them has its own style of government, with its own plans and policies. While one country may favour nature conservation, another may push for major development of its resources.

Another problem is that the seats of government for most of these countries lie a long way south of the Arctic in capital cities like Washington and Moscow. When politicians take decisions for their countries, the remote Arctic territory may be far from their minds. Greenland is owned by Denmark but has its own parliament. The parliament has a say in development decisions which will affect the people of Greenland, who are mostly Inuit. Partly because of this, Greenland Inuit still lead a more traditional way of life than the North American Inuit, whose lifestyle has changed dramatically.

◄
Melting icebergs are silhouetted against light from the midnight sun in King Oscar fiord, Greenland. Unless the Arctic is protected, such places will continue to be polluted and ruined.

A scientist wears a surgical mask and gloves as he removes an ice core sample from the drill that has extracted it from the ice. This avoids contaminating the sample before it is analysed in the laboratory.

CONSERVATION

Some governments' decisions have been good for the Arctic. Alaska now has a dozen national parks, created to protect the state's special wildlife and delicate habitats. Conservation is a popular theme in Norway, Sweden and Finland, and national parks protect parts of the northern forest and tundra in these countries.

In Russia, conservation has been less of a priority. This massive country is picking up the pieces after the break-up of the Soviet Union. At the moment, it faces a great pressure just to feed and provide work for its huge population. However, the conservation movement is growing in Russia, and environmentalists are campaigning to protect the Arctic from overdevelopment and pollution.

WORKING TOGETHER

Arctic countries are now working together to protect the environment and its wildlife. For example, in 1973, five countries joined together to protect polar bears, which were under threat from hunting and habitat destruction. Norway, USSR, Canada, USA and Denmark agreed to protect the bears' habitat and migration routes. Unfortunately, levels of the poisonous chemicals, PCBs, are increasing very quickly in polar bears. If PCB pollution of the Arctic continues, polar bears will contain enough PCBs to be classified as toxic waste by 2005. Their future does not look bright.

Researchers from many different countries are also working together to help to protect the Arctic in the future. A team of European scientists is probing deep into the ice in Greenland and taking huge ice core samples. These will tell them what the atmosphere was like as far back as 500,000 years ago. Greenland's ice is a frozen record of dust particles and chemicals that were in the atmosphere in the past. The scientists hope these ice cores will help them to understand climate changes that are happening now, so they can predict changes in the future.

An Inuit technician releases a helium-filled weather balloon into the Canadian Arctic air to test the atmosphere for pollution.

The Arctic is a wild and inhospitable environment but it is also fragile. It must be protected if it is not to be damaged by human activity.

Another team of scientists from Europe, the USA, Japan, Russia and New Zealand have worked on the European Arctic Stratospheric Ozone Experiment (EASOE). From November 1991 to March 1992, they collected data from weather balloons and from ground stations, to find out precisely how and why ozone is being destroyed over the Arctic. Their findings should help the world to find the best way to stop the destruction of the ozone layer.

But there is an even greater hope for the Arctic and its peoples. Recently, the eight Arctic countries have come together to protect the unique Arctic environment. In June 1991, the governments of USA, Canada, Russia, Finland, Sweden, Denmark, Norway and Iceland pledged their support for the protection of the Arctic from outside air and marine pollution. This is a major step forward and it is to be hoped that, by acting together, these countries will be stronger and better able to protect their Arctic land.

GRASS-ROOTS ACTION

Action at national and international level is vital to protect the Arctic. But local people, who live there and depend on the Arctic, should also play an important part in protecting their environment. After all, they are the ones who can see the changes happening around them, which affect their lifestyle and the environment they depend on. In Canada and Greenland there are now Inuit Brotherhoods. These are organizations of local people, who fight against changes that would harm their traditional culture.

Many local people are fiercely proud of their homeland and take action if they see it is under threat. The Saami in northern Norway are a good illustration of this. In 1979, the Norwegian government proposed to build a new hydroelectric power scheme, with a dam that would cross the Alta Valley in the mountainous far north. The scheme would have flooded a huge area where reindeer breed, and would have disturbed rivers in which salmon spawn.

Reindeer and salmon are both an important part of the traditional Saami lifestyle.

The Saami believed that the government was destroying their culture and the heart of their land. So Saami farmers and fishermen, conservation groups and many other people formed a resistance campaign called the *Folksaksjon* (People's Action). By late 1980, the movement had over 20,000 members and their motto, 'The River Shall Live' won the hearts and minds of fellow Scandinavians and other people in Europe. After about two years of bitter dispute, the government finally backed down. It realized that it had pushed the development of this remote Saami area too far. It had put the need to generate electricity above the traditional way of life of the Saami.

Battles like this one are happening all over the world – the resistance to the Canadian HEP scheme in Quebec (see page 33) is another example. In the Arctic, as elsewhere, more and more people now realize that it is important to allow room for wildlife and to protect the natural environment. Individuals, pressure groups and even governments are calling for a new respect for the natural world, and for peoples who live close to nature, like the rainforest Amerindians, or traditional Inuit. If we put our ideas into practice, it can make a difference to the world around us – and that includes the beautiful world of the Arctic.

GLOSSARY

Algae Tiny plants that live in water.

Baleen The plates of flexible horn-like tissue that grow in the mouths of filter-feeding whales.

Carnivore A meat-eating animal.

Conservation Protecting the natural environment.

DDT Dichlorodiphenyl-trichloroethane. A man-made insecticide used against insect pests of crops. It is highly poisonous and banned from use in many countries.

Ecosystems The relationships between plants and animals, and their habitats.

Environment A term to describe the conditions in which a plant or an animal lives. This can include the amount of light, cold, heat, and water there is, and what other plants and animals there are.

Exploit To take advantage of a resource, sometimes to excess.

Fossil fuels The remains of plants and animals that lived millions of years ago, which have changed to become oil, gas and coal.

Groundwater Water that is found underground in the soil or in rock cavities.

Habitat The place where a plant or animal lives, such as woodland, a pond, or the seashore.

Ice cap A large area of permanent ice.

Immunity The body's natural resistance to disease.

Inhospitable Harsh and difficult to live in.

Migration The seasonal movement of animals between two areas, caused by their search for food and breeding areas.

Nomads People who move from pasture to pasture during the year in search of grazing for their animals or food, sometimes following animal migrations.

PCBs Polychlorinated biphenyls. A group of man-made compounds used in the electrical and plastics industries. PCBs are highly poisonous and banned in many countries.

Pollutants Chemicals that harm the environment, either immediately, or because they build up over a period of time.

Quota A limited allowance of something.

Radioactivity The giving out of radiation, which is harmful to plants and animals in large doses.

Resources Materials, plants and animals that we can make use of.

Zooplankton Tiny animals that drift, mainly on the surface, of the oceans. They include the larvae of crabs and fish eggs.

·BOOKS TO READ·

Conserving the Polar Regions, Barbara James (Wayland 1990).

Give Me My Father's Body, Kenn Harper (Blacklead, 1986). The story of an Inuit boy taken to the USA by explorers.

Inuit, Bryan and Cherry Alexander (Wayland 1992).

Living Arctic, Hugh Brody (Faber and Faber 1987).

Living Arctic wallcharts, available from Pictorial Charts Educational Trust, 27 Kirchden Rd, London W13 0UD.

Polar Regions, David Lambert (Wayland 1987).

Polar Regions, Terry Jennings (Oxford University Press 1986).

Saami of Lapland, Piers Vitebsky (Wayland 1993).

·USEFUL ADDRESSES·

Information about the indigenous peoples of the Arctic is available from:

Indigenous Survival International
Suite 300, 47 Clarence St
Ottawa, Ontario K1N 9K1

Minority Rights Group
379 Brixton Rd
London SW9 7DE

Survival International
310 Edgeware Rd
London W2 1DY

Tungavik Federation of Nunavut
Suite 800, 130 Slater St
Ottawa, Ontario K1P 6E2

Tusarliivik
Greenland Home Rule
Information Service
PO Box 1020
DK 3900 Nuuk
Greenland

More information about the Arctic environment is available from:

Friends of the Earth

Australia:
366 Smith St
Collingwood
Victoria 3065

Britain:
26–28 Underwood Street
London N1 7AQ

Canada:
Suite 53, 54 Queen St
Ottawa KP 5C5

New Zealand:
Nagal House, Courthouse Lane
PO Box 39/065
Auckland West

Greenpeace

Australia:
310 Angas St
Adelaide 5000

Britain:
30-31 Islington St
London N1 8XE

Canada:
427 Bloor St West
Toronto, Ontario

New Zealand:
Private Bag
Wellesley St
Auckland

INDEX

Numbers in **bold** refer to pages where illustrations appear or are captioned.